Second Wind; Second Sight

SECOND WIND; SECOND SIGHT

Joan Finnigan

BLACK MOSS PRESS

BMP

1998

Published by Black Moss Press, 2450 Byng Road, Windsor, Ontario N8W 3E8. Black Moss Press books are distributed by Firefly Books, 3680 Victoria Park Ave., Willowdale, Ontario, M2H 3K1. All orders should be directed there.

Black Moss Press would like to acknowledge the support of the Department of Canadian Heritage.

We would also like to acknowledge the support of the Canada Council for the Arts for our publishing program.

Canadian Cataloguing in Publication Data

Finnigan, Joan, 1925-
    Second Wind; Second Sight

I. Title.

PS8511.I55S33 1998   C811'.54   C98-900981-5
PR9199.3.F46S33 1998

∧ Cover photo by Joan Finnigan; design by John Doherty.

Millhaven Creek; Sydenham, Ont

CONTENTS

For
Jonathan & Helen, Roderick & Margaret, Martha & Louis;
and their children:
Matthew, Caitlin & Maria; Iain & Maura;
Geneviéve & MacKenzie.

—from Hambly Lake, 1994-1998

Poetry. This collection of poetry. The why, the how, and the where-to. I first began writing poetry when I was nine. At least, that is the first documentation of the abnormality. It may have emerged before that but nothing has survived in paper evidence deposited at Queen's University Archives. In pre-pubescence and puberty I used to get up in the middle of the night and write "great lines" in the dark on pages of a black-covered scribbler kept for this purpose. At this stage of my life I don't pretend that this nocturnal phenomenon was a manifestation of precocity but more likely, I think, a sign of childhood disturbance, even a symptom of communication needs unfulfilled.

"Creativity is the most positive defense of the damaged individual." I have been writing poetry ever since and it remains my primary steadfast genre. But I can no more say today why I do it than I could back then. Over the decades I have made various attempts to tackle the why of it, in essays and particularly in my ongoing manuscript, Aphorisms and Absolutes. "All art is a failed experiment." Or, "A poem is because I would like to share part of my soul." Or, "The artist is always in pain; but he has learned the metaphysical process of making gold out of dross."

Back in 1970 when you could still get a good poetry anthology for $2.95 from Mel Hurtig, Naim Kattan then of the Canada Council, enunciated for me something I had been groping to put into words at the time. He said that it seemed to him that "there are two kinds of writers—those who write out of need and those who write out of the fullness of life." He said it to me at a time when I had come close to making the same observation myself, and about myself as a poet particularly. I had identified the invitations to the muse, the essential sense of wellbeing, even the feeling of "belonging to the universe" which precedes my poetic process. To write a good poem I have to be transfused with the rooted tranquillity of trees.

In over half a century of living and creating, not much has changed really. I am still predominantly interested in writing, and reading, something that has been created out of the fullness and richness of life. True, I have on occasions written poems arising out of anger and negativism. But they are not my best. They may be clever, satirical, humorous, even parodies as "Poems for the New Tyranny," but they are not the kind of poems which might grow to become part of the soul philosophy of people.

If I cannot tell you so much about the way perhaps I can tell you a little more about the how. Generally speaking my poems tend to be people-inspired, ("Who Cares? Who Cares?" "The Stone Picker"), event-inspired ("My Father Often Told Me"), love-inspired ("Salute, Polar Bear Pass"). Sometimes single lines imbed themselves in me, echo in mysterious chambers, lines like, "Everyone knows you are my blind spot," which came out of hiding in "Confession;" "He thought the moon only shone over Ireland," which I know, sometime, like a virus incubating, will out; "Old age is fantasy land," which I felt would emerge in "At the Kingston Shopping-Centre," but didn't.

Even the title for this collection was people-inspired and incubated for a period. I was visiting my optometrist here in Kingston, being fitted for new glasses. He is from the Ottawa Valley so, naturally we got into the storytelling in the course of which he talked about some old people getting "second sight." This led me to an association with the experience of second wind which I used to invite or expect when I was young and dancing all night; or the second wind my father talked of in overtime hockey games in the NHL. Second wind is perhaps more applicable as an image for the young and active; second sight more symbolic for the inward-turning contemplative philosophical stance of old age, that time, when all things being in accord, intelligence should turn into wisdom.

But our later years are not necessarily without second, or even third wind that might bless us through change, and risk, and growth, wrought by new friends, new relationships, and the joy of becoming part of the lives of our grandchildren. "For My Grandchildren" is, I hope, a celebration and an evocation of the loving beyond ourselves which is granted to the fortunate amongst us towards the end of our lives.

Oftentimes these days I feel like a tree still standing alone on a hillside after clear cutting, enduring the deaths around me of parents, brothers, relatives, friends--. "Winter Walk," "Last Mission," are part of the grieving, perhaps the second wind that comes after grieving, as well as being part of the second sight which renders all those enlightenments and reassessments after the death of a loved one. Yes, even the death of a loved one is part of the fullness of life.

Of all the literary genres, I believe drama and poetry remain the most cathartic for the audience. I mean that in the Greek sense; purging emotions. Healthy people express their emotions on the site. When they are angry they yell it out immediately. When they are hurt, they turn at once upon the hurt inflictor. When they have grief they weep until the time for weeping is done. Unhealthy people fail to have this mechanism for salvation; they have to find outlets, sublimations, substitutes in many places, many ways, including art. Hence the value of art, all art, as positive surrogate for the real thing.

But no matter what subconsciously motivates, disclosure of one's heart and soul and being is therapeutic for the writer as well. Indeed, I have long suspected that the artist is an individual who could not identify with either father or mother and so must move through the centre to recreate his own world.

Just as I believe that every aware teacher, daily, has to be congnizant of the fact that what he says and does, one word, one act, may change or influence a child's life, so, I believe every serious writer must be constantly conscious of the responsibility he bears in a parallel way to self-disclosure with honesty and integrity.

In his generative book, The Transparent Self, Sydney M. Jouard expressed this better than I;

"Authentic writing is psychedelic for the reader – `it turns him on' – in ways that we do not fully understand, at least in a scientific sense, the disclosed experience of the other person enables us to see things, feel things, imagine things, hope for things that we could never even have imagined before we were exposed to the revelations of the discloser. The vicarious experience that reading or listening provides can shape our essence, change us, just as first hand experience can."

It would, therefore, by my humble hope that some of the poems in Second Wind; Second Sight, being part of the quintessence of my heart and soul and being, will impact, as a kind of loving, on the heart and soul and being of someone out there.

And that's the whereto.

SUMMER STORM

In my childhood on my Radford grandfather's farm
summer thunderstorms allowed no one to sleep,
not my night-prowling young uncles,
not the hired men,
not even me, Little Jumping Joan.

Summerstorms, it was always said, were sent
from the mountains on the Ontario side of the River
into the pure Irish bailiwicks of Western Quebec,
lambasting, psychopathic, annihilating
Canadian rains out of the guts of the universe
with lightning flattening the good grain,
setting the hay barns on fire,
striking dead the hired men
sheltering under the elm trees
in the farm fields,
taking down windmills,
snapping off lightning rods,
sending the women into fiddlings of fear
and recitations of all the Deaths
by Lightning occurring in the Valley
for the last hundred years
on both sides of the River

Valley rain was not the soft civilized rain
of Ireland, fairy-footed, caressing
forty shades of green, tapping
at Queen Maeve's tomb
on top of Knocknarea.

Valley rain was not an Irish rain
gently falling through court tombs,
ruined castles and monasteries,
gently pelting O'Rourke's Table
and the lovers last picnic there
before Diarmid MacMurrough came
to carry off Dervorgilla.

No, it was the savage rain
of a big adolescent half-grown country
and in my Valley clan the women went haywire,
especially if the storm came at night:
I had one evangelical aunt who used
to rouse everyone in the house,
seat them at the kitchen table
and lead them in prayer
for the duration of the storm,
raising her arms heavenwards,
at every clap of thunder,
every bolt of lightning
yelling "Hallelujah!"

In my childhood on my Radford grandfather's farm
summer thunderstorms allowed no one to sleep,
not my night-prowling young uncles,
not the hired men,
not even me, Little Jumping Joan.

MY FATHER OFTEN TOLD ME

My father often told me
that when he was a child in wintertimes
the snow drifted so high he used
to go out through the door
on the upstairs verandah of his house
to get to school

whenever we went back to visit the clans
—and we often did—
he showed me the house of his childhood
and I believed him when I was very young,
just as I believed in Santa Claus and God,
and the world of the Twelve Dancing Princesses

then when I got older and wiser,
about nine or ten or eleven,
and he told his stories
about the super-dog family dog,
Jock who could close the door after himself
and put down his own newspapers,
I heard my mother poo-poo him,
tell him, "shut up, you old fool!
you're full of malarkey,"
and I began to doubt him

then when I got very wise and experienced,
about fifteen or sixteen,
and had discovered that God
didn't answer prayers,

that princes didn't arrive,
that Santa Claus did not
come down the chimney,
I came to believe that my father
was a liar, a teller of untrue tales,
a spinner of improbable yarns

and I went through a period of hating
my father, of questioning everything
he did, of not believing a word he said,
of having all the answers myself

but still, sometimes, visiting the clans,
I would look at the upstairs verandah
on the house of his childhood
and measure the distance to the ground
where he walked to school

and then when I married and had children
my father suddenly became wiser,
and I listened to him telling me truths
that changed my life;

as I began to learn about drifts
and great storms and cruel winds
always in your face
that could make the road impassable,
I looked at the house and the verandah anew
and I saw that, yes, indeed, the north wind
in a winter storm could move
across the fields untrammelled
for miles and days
and pile the snow as high
as the legend-maker's measure

my father lived long enough to recognize
his mistakes and know there was nothing
he could do about them; and so we became
real friends and I realized
there was always a basis for the legends
he told so often and with such delight
as my mother frowned her disapproval;
she knew great stories, too,
but she hoarded them all inside her
and took them with her to the grave

such is the cycle of all our legends;
from the special event recalled and retold,
through the time of the disbelievers
and disclaimers, to the weaving
of the story into the culture
of the people

the house is still there
and the verandah is still there
and the winters still come
in the Ottawa Valley
with winds from the north
that pile the snow in drifts
as high as the storyteller's eye

For My Grandchildren

Foremost, I wish for you parents who know
that love is a discipline, that without love
there is no discipline, and that without discipline
there is no love

I wish you such laughter that,
anyone hearing your laughter, will surely know
that you are well-loved

I wish you parents whose caring for each other
is a constantly becoming partners, better friends,
greater lovers, a living example for you
of loving with all its unspoken and unrevealed
unexpectedly articulated and acted out

I do not wish for you the populist superficialities
like good looks or remarkable I.Q.s,
athletic prowess, entertainment talent,
great ambition and drive;

I want for you emotional health
passed on to you so that
you can layer your precious lifetime
with mysterious riches, change and grow,
grow and change, shed skins, begin again,
knowing always when the time has come

I wish for you a complete childhood,
not one cut short by use, abuse, favouritism,
over-protection, rejection, negative criticism,
power-motivated confrontations,
threats unfulfilled, promises unkept,
forced baby-sitting of younger siblings,
(making you into that most vulnerable,
most crippled of beings,
the mother or father surrogate),
unrealistic self-destroying goals
presented by parents to whom
the same destructive things happened,
by parents who have not been granted
(by their parents before them)
the insight and courage to change
and break the sick patterns, to make
something better happen for their children.

"Christ! What are patterns for!"[1]
For every child is born good and honest,
just, moral, righteous, creative, trusting,
and it is given to the abysmal evil
of bad parenting to damage and destroy
all that.

I do not wish for you wealth nor even
luxurious living leading to the soul's denigration;
ruthlessly, I do not even wish you escape
from pain, stress, hunger;
I only wish that you be gifted the proper tools
to deal with these throughout your lives

I do not wish you "success" in its present-day definitions;
career power, money power, political power, feminist power,
for "where love rules there is no will to power,
and where power predominates, there love is lacking."[2]

Yes, I wish your success to be
Zen in the art of living!

Foremost I want emotional health for you
so that, despite the shifting sands of relationships,
the cumulative cankers of disappointments,
the pain of losses like open wounds in your side,
you will still be able to expand your joy
in the challenge of living fully,
(as I now, at seventy, can tally
all these things, bear their burdens
and yet proclaim my joy
in your presence upon the earth,
and in your unlimited unfolding potential)

I wish for you from the very beginning
parents who will stand on guard to protect
your self-respect, your self-image, your self-pride,
who will recognize and develop
your embryonic talents and gifts,
cultivate your imagination,
nurture your inborn creativity;

I wish for you parents who,
when you drag in the dead snake
will not cry out in horror
but tell you the folk tale,
demonstrate the chain of connections,
defend animals as works of art,
achieve permanency for your "Innocent Eye."[3]

I wish for you, my grandchildren,
to grow up with an unerring sense
to ferret out everything phoney,
hypocritical, dishonest;
commercial entrapments, materialistic values,
social climbers, people who tell lies
and worse still, live lies,
things gone to plastic and gimmickry,
technology become a sick simulation

I would wish for you as little as possible
to do with modern technology
and technological changes
(and as much as possible to do with love)
for "technological change alters not only habits
of life, but patterns of thought and valuation."[4]

"The Chinese sage Tzu-Gung was travelling the country north of the River Han when he saw an old man making an irrigation ditch by descending into a well with a vessel, fetching it up and pouring the water out into his ditch. Tzu-Gung explained to him the mechanics of the wooden lever and how it would speed up his labour. Then anger rose in the old man's face and he said to the Chinese sage, `I have heard my teacher say that whoever uses machines does all his work like a machine. He who does his work like a machine grows a heart like a machine, and he who carries the heart of a machine in his breast loses his simplicity. He who has lost his simplicity becomes unsure in the strivings of his soul. Uncertainty in the strivings of the soul is something which does not agree with honest sense. It is not that I do not know of such things; I am ashamed to use them'."[5]

I would wish for you to grow up counting not your money
but your values, doing a regular stocktaking
not of blue-chip securities but of principles
for in order to meet the tempter, the con man,
the beguiler you have to have your philosophy internalized
in your heart, in your genes, like monogamy;
the ancient tribal trickster is always
at your elbow plotting how to mislead you
out of living your life fully, and with worth.

I would wish for you a fully-protected curiosity
so that you can become the naturalist, the explorer,
the discoverer with ears to hear plants
growing in the night,
with eyes to see a dream-bed
in the prairie dark,
finding out what we've undone
so that we can mend the earth,
so that you can mend the earth
we've undone

I wish for you the endowment of simplicity
in your life, the formula to find
the horsepower of a waterfall,
the methodology to grow pine from seed.
the patience to wait
for the bread to rise.

Predominately, I would wish for you the power of love;
female love is power, male love is power and I would wish
for you NO other kind of power for the poor denuded earth
cannot bear any other kinds of power; industrialization,
mass production, monopolies, planned obsolescence,
all the corrupted forms of power which are destroying
the earth, YOUR earth.

Archimedes once said,
"Give me a place to stand
and I will move the world."

And, behold, in the late 1990s, Rogers, the Canadian monopolist of technological change, having bought "the place to stand," then said to the about-to-be deprived and impoverished Canadians, "I will stand on your eyes, your ears, your nerves, your brain, and the world will move in any tempo and pattern I choose, for surely the CRTC is in the palm of my hand."

I would wish for you, my grandchildren,
the ability to smile so that anyone,
seeing your smiles, will know instantly
that you are the cherished of the earth,
and therefore can cherish the earth.

I would wish you, my grandchildren, creativity
and imagination in everything you touch,
to provide the levitation of your spirit
and ongoing contact with your soul,
a real counteraction to technology gone wild;
I would wish for you an unerring nose for ersatz
and idiotic misuse of the earth's
precious and dwindling resources

"Among his most recent research projects, Dr. Diddley, a computer professor, is developing increasingly more convincing virtual reality displays, including one for an otherwise stationary bicycle that riders can pedal and steer through computer-generated, three-dimensional scenery projected on tiny video screens inside a special helmet—."

I would wish for you trees, and more trees
more affinity with the magic of trees
for "whoever is rooted in the soil endures."6
I would wish for you a lifelong communication
with the earth, nature, instinct, intuition
for these are the touchstones, compasses, lifelines
to an authentic well-lived life

I would wish for you parents who will quantify
your sense of beauty (so that, one day, like me,
approaching seventy, beckoned by the path to the lake
after a bunting snowfall, you will take time
to walk abroad, glorying in it all, and thanking
your parents for their gift of life
that makes it possible for you to experience
the winter's day).

As I have always had in my lifetime,
I would wish for you the heritage
of a beloved landscape
that becomes your allegiance, your nationality,
so that loving neighbourhoods join hands
to become loving communities, regions,
intent upon preserving the earth,
our home.

Finally, I would wish for you
the nobility of self-actualization;
"Become what thou art!" as Nietzsche cried
Well-loved emotionally healthy people
become self-actualizers,
challenge the unknown,
embrace the universe,

love themselves as others,
hove to honesty,
cleave to their own code of ethics,
maintain their child-like spontaneity,
simplicity and naturalness,
choose philosophical lives of service,
are ruled by their own character
rather than by the rules of society
choose co-operativeness over competition,
become synergic rather than antagonistic,
wholly embody creativity,
and out of their own healthiness,
choose healthy people to love

And I would wish for you
the grace of self-actualization,
a triumph of living,
and then I would wish you
the joyous spontaneous dispossessing loving
that comes to self-actualizing lovers,
and then the committed fruitful monogamous mating
that comes to self-actualizing partners.
"For together two is more than two; alone, one is less than one.
Alone one expends time and energy substituting, making up
for the absence or loss of other."7

I would wish for you strength for the battle
but not so much that you attract leaners;
I would wish for you courage
but not so much that you waste it
fighting unworthy wars;
I would wish you character, moral sense,
the one to enable you to risk and change,
the other to preserve your human dignity.

I would wish you
membership in the Aquarian Conspiracy.

"The mind, which sometimes presumes to believe
that there is no such thing as a miracle,
is itself a miracle."[8]

Still I would never want you to lose
your profound humanness to blindered intellectualism
your survival instincts to woolly abstractions,
your birthright intuitions
to orthodoxy and dehumanizing institutionalizations.
I would wish for you maturation,
serendipity, integration
and re-discovery of God

I would wish for you time to grow old,
and finish the tapestry of your life,
embroider wisdom into your grandchildren's lives.

I would wish for you the ultimate grace
of being able to love those around you
beyond yourself

finally, out of your consummate healthiness,
I would wish for you the apogee,
the mystic experience
of belonging to the universe
for "the most beautiful thing we can experience
is the mysterious. It is the source of all art
and science."[9]

RINK

Yes, my grandchildren, when he was born,
a Blue Baby in the fabulous Twenties,
the heart specialist removed his stethoscope
from the tiny, pale, heaving chest,
pronounced to the suspended parents,
"This little lad will never paly hockey.
An enlarged heart. Perhaps six months--."

Out of Ottawa and into the pure clear air
of the Upper Pontiac, she and her mother,
with all the old-time rural remedies,
breathed into the child the breath of life,
love, stronger than the inchoate heart
of primitive stars,
belief, deeper than cosmic infinity,
refusing death's entry.

Just to prove that doctors
are not really gods,
he was on the backyard rink
by age three, double-edged skates
and miniature hockey stick, custom-forged
in his father's national arena of glory,
the old Ottawa Senators' Auditorium.

His undauntable damaged heart
would not let him play fast forward,
but his great eyes and genetic reflexes
marked out for him his permanent place
in goal.

Road hockey, pond hockey, pick-up hockey,
river hockey, backyard hockey,
in simulation of his All-Star father,
he played his time-bomb heart
into the local annals of courage,
when Glashan rink gates were locked
even climbed the chain-link fence,
fifteen feet high,
with his skates on,
to join the pick-up team
on Saturday mornings

Stood at night with his ear lugs down,
thirty below zero, hose in hand,
swinging smooth steady waters
onto the perennial backyard rink
at his own house, no girls allowed
to scratch and mess up the ice,
soften the atmosphere

Dedicated, determined, pig-headed
like his father and fathers before him,
as his enlarging heart grew
it humped his teenage back,
but augmented his courage,
so sorely needed when his younger brother
went on to join the ranks of Junior A

In the wartime Forties,
still rejecting his destiny,
to be closer to the game he adored
(and the faltering father
he still worshipped)

he moved to a wider rink,
up and down the stairs
of the old Ottawa Auditorium,
(his faulty heart working hard,
fighting gravity) where he sold
hockey programmes while his father
scored on the ice below
for an ailing Air Force Team

When he died at age thirty
in the arms of the old hockey player,
right above Canada
God made the first rink in heaven,
put up golden goal-posts,
blew the opening whistle
on an eternal hockey game.

WHO CARES? WHO CARES?

Yes, my grandchildren, I once knew a man who threw
money out of the windows of celebrated hotels
like the Royal York, yelling "Who cares? Who cares?"
from Halifax to Ottawa to Calgary he tossed
one hundred dollar bills out to the squealing,
shoving obsequious masses, laughing like a towering Zeus
clowning in Olympian heaven, down the tarmacs,
at the railway stations, from city core taxis,
through the streets of his little town,
laughing and roaring, "Who cares? Who cares?"

He had carved out Canadian identity, laying down
transcontinental tracks, leading armies of men
through muskeg, blue-tongued snows, winds and mosquitoes
from proper hell, his drive their compass,
arriving at the last spike early, sharing
the contract bonuses with his men, the sons of Martha.

His wife, upstaged by railways, dams and New York subways,
moved into a suite at the Park Plaza,
blew a fortune on Bloor Street, ended her pain
with an accommodating Players cigarette.

Loveless, childless, the giant railway genius
bound himself over to a man named Johnny Walker,
and, as given to some of us, grew wiser
as his death approached and the Income Tax men
pounded on his door, decided to give it all away
rather than have the government take it.

Men died for him, and he died alone,
with little left of the fortune
that had separated him from love,
without anyone to look upon his frailties
with forgiveness, and no one ever to answer
his impoverished cry for help,
"Who cares? Who cares?"

The Stone Picker

Yes, my grandchildren, there was once upon a time
in the Ottawa Valley a famous school teacher,
Singing Bridie Conway of back of Brudenell,
(fittingly named for the general who led
the Charge of the Light Brigade)
who taught in her one-room schoolhouse
five generations of Irish along the Opeongo Line,
first settlement road, and the place
Where We All Began

In the pedagogical traces Singing Bridie was
until she reached the age of seventy-six,
had saved not only her retirement fund,
but her burying money as well.

For sixty years in that one-room schoolhouse,
grades one to eight, Entrance included,
she coddled the legends, reheated the folk-tales,
preserved the language, passed down the songs,
sang them in the morning and at night
on her way to and from that one-room schoolhouse,
sang them just as her ten brothers sang them,
working the hilly hundred acres
of their ancestral farm, sang them
en route to and from her boarding-house,
thirty dollars a month, for one room again,
where the stove-pipe ran up through
from the general store below,
and her window looked out to the Opeongo Hills,
a diurnal perspective on her clouding hopes,
and eclipsing dreams.

For sixty years all winter long,
under the barrier snows,
more beautiful than despair,
the immigrant leprechauns,
tossed and heaved the stones
around and about
the Opeongo fields and clearings,
all the better, 'twas said,
to hide their crocks of gold.

By spring every Opeongo farm,
Conways included,
had seeded a new crop
of picaresque pebbles,
delinquent rocks;
the ploughed earth
lay in bondage again

And every summer when school ended,
Singing Bridie Conway, dutiful daughter,
returned to the ancestral fields
and there picked stones all summer long
until her hands were as raw and bloody
as the curses in her mouth.

CHRISTMAS MESSAGE

This morning I got up
needing to nurture a prayer for you

No. I awoke thinking first about trees
and their place in the universe

in the winds of who
and the stars of why

now, without fanfare, the snow
is moving its moccasined battalions
up over the ramparts of the city
whiting out the neons that keep you
from finding out what yours eyes can see,
the push-buttons that keep you
from finding out what yours hands can do,
and the computers that keep you
from finding out what your mind can do

the snow is moving its ghostly legions
up from the river and over the city

now I need to nurture
a prayer for you

"Peace to those in far and dangerous places.
Peace to those in safe surrounding places,"

and the voices of the angels
from last night's Christmas Concert
still drown out the super-jets
stumbling through snowflakes
in the polluted skies;
when the snow came up from the river
it found the mountains sleeping

in the sacramental silences of the snow
the carolling voices of the children
from last night's Christmas Concert

sweeten and swell in the winds of who
and up and over the erosions of Bethlehem
follow the stars of why

"Peace to those in far and dangerous places.
Peace to those in safe surrounding places."

The Meaning of Meaning

A renowned British astro-physicist,
irritated by anyone claiming
to "know the mind of God,"
or "see the face of God,"
has publicly chastised
in a national newspaper
a man called Hawking

Dr Michael Rowan-Robinson,
professor at Imperial College, London,
has proof that life has no meaning
and wants Hawking to know it
in front of everyone
in the country

no matter, of course, that Hawking
although divinely impaired,
has jousted with the mystery,
and changed the theory
of the universe

no matter that
when a Canada Goose falls
wounded from the sky,
two of his flock
descend and stay by his side
until he either recuperates
or dies

no matter that
my love for my grandchildren
gives cumulative meaning
to my life;
and will to theirs
as they mark their stars

with as much illumination
and intelligent insight
as given to the astro-physicist
in his wholly scientific search
for no meaning

which gives his whole life meaning.

THE WIND LADY

Yes, my grandchildren, there was once
a lady in myth-making Montpelier
who never went out of the house
if the wind was blowing

My friend, Mary of old, tells me
that she had a relative in New England
who never went out of her house
when the wind was blowing

Now my friend, Mary of old,
has had some ridiculous relatives -
there was the grand-uncle one who spent
all of his millions in riotous living
before he died so his children
couldn't inherit and "be spoiled";
he thought riotous living
would kill him off early,
but it didn't. Instead he lived
to be ninety-nine and damn near
ran out of money for himself!

And then there were her two maiden aunts
who used to lock up any male callers
in their root cellar, keep them there
until they promised to stop drinking,
signed the WCTU pledge.

And that spinster cousin, a theatre-fanatic,
cursed with neuralgia in the face,
rheumatism in the knee-bones,
and arthritis in the thigh-bones,
who, for the last twenty years of her long life
appeared at every theatre event
in historic Kingston with a draw-string
bagful of shawls. As the play progressed
she unravelled from the bag
her knee-shawl, her hip-shawl
and, if truly chilled,
her head-shawl.

But really! A relative who never went
out of her house when the wind
was blowing! What could have brought
this strange behaviour upon her?
What could have caused this corruption
of a natural revelling in nature?

Had some tornado torn her hair out
at the roots when she was young?
Had some fulmine wind fanned the farm
where she lived and the lightning struck
before her very eyes some sibling
dead at the foot of a tree?
What had she learned from the wind
that was so ill, so prevailing
that she hid forever after in the house?
In her sixth sense, so heightened by fear,
did she hear foreboding rolling towards her,
foretelling riding Aeolus through the trees?
Did she hear something dire in the wind
and try to wind-proof the straight-jacket
of her psyche?

If she never went out when the wind
was blowing, how did she know from inside
the wind was cornering the house?
Did the windows rattle and the trees bend
and the smoke blow back down the chimney
to warn her to stay inside
for the wind was loose and abroad,
blowing stars from their black mountains,
throwing dapplings through the sunlight,
stacking snowdrifts along the Milky Way.

I ask you, how can you stay alive anywhere
on the earth and escape the wind?
The ultramundane wind? The linguist wind?
The charged and changing wind?
Why, it would be like fleeing an enemy
who could read your mind and see your soul.

And then I think of my mother
who hated the wind, remembering
on a summer's day in afternoon nap time
when the wind on a marathon blew down
from the Opeongo Hills, across the Ottawa,
through the fields of my ancestral
and beleaguered land,
rattling the green window blinds
in the great cool kitchen
of my maternal grandparents,

Remembering that land-sailing wind,
premonitive of a future emptiness
in all those childhood rooms,
I better understand the roots
of my mother's hatred of the wind.

Past all the departures and deaths,
she braved the wind. Would to all
the wind-gods I could tell the story,
the full story of how she braved the winds!

Oh, my grandchildren, can you imagine
a lady who never left her house
if the wind was blowing?

I ask you,
when is the wind not blowing
around some corner of the earth?
Why I've even known some winds
so harsh and vengeful they blew
through the thin coffins
in the country graveyards,
ruffled the hair of the dead
lying there, thinking they had finally
escaped from the willy-willy,
were safely out of wind's way.

SALUTE

When I helped her back
from the bathroom on her walker,
breathlessly she fell
onto her chair by the window
which looks no longer
out on the landscape of her garden,
but backwards into the inscape
of her too long life

Oh, God only knows what memories
and dried-out dreams she rotates there
behind her blind brown eyes,
how many of her living
and her dead she hears now
in the memory drums
of her deaf ears

(in the end we are all bound together
by something as fragile
and ephemeral as memories)

"I can't do anything now,
anything at all," she wails
to me in a tiny voice
that matches her tiny fading tears
of frustration

I pat her on the head and say,
"Never mind, my mother,
you have done wonders in your time,
you have done wonders."

And she leans forward a moment,
"Who's that?" she asks.
"Who's that?"

And I tell her again

Now, back home and distanced
from her and her dissolution,
I hope she will die soon
just sitting in her chair
by the blind window,
slip off into some pleasant dream
her life never accomplished,

into some memory of love,
of her children gathered
in joyous summer picnics
around her,
of her husband coming home
in the days before he broke
her heart

I pray she will deny her genes,
avoid the long drawn-out agony
of stroke that will close off
even her voice,
leave her vegetating on a hospital bed
in a sterile womb of dark silence,
picking at the bed-clothes

Back home
I pray she will go soon
before we all forget
what a classy, beautiful woman
she once was, full of grit
and energy

tiger-mother going off to tackle
the teachers on Parents' Nights
at the schools

dividing the spoils
amongst the bill collectors

putting the lid down
on the piano lessons
and the piano

covering her retreat

potential wasted,
like oil-spill
polluting her whole universe,

as she tried to keep
the unkeepable promises

POLAR BEAR PASS

Because I couldn't rescue my brother
(although I am my brother's keeper),
I'd like to go to Polar Bear Pass
in the high Arctic where the animals
are not yet afraid of man,
to some clean pure world
of life at the starting-gate

Because I loved and understood him,
I'd like him to rise and go with me
together make a pilgrimage
to the Canadian Compostela,
to sanctified Bathurst Island,
where he could hold a wild ptarmigan
in his warm hands at the world's end,
glow a smile of inward joy and love,
incandescence from within his soul.

Because his life was so filled with pain,
I'd like to think of him now
in some sacramental landscape
where the wolves look in the windows,
where the musk ox graze upon the doorsteps,
where the polar bear push past
the Lookout Tower, pose for the cameras

Behind the pop carolling,
the commercial glitz,
the glutinous food ads,
the political insanity
and chaos of our country,
I'd like to be with him again,
watch him put up
his beloved Christmas tree
in the sanctity of a preserve
where man has not yet
learned to fear man.

NEW YEARS EVE WIDOWLAND

Here it comes again,
   New Year's Eve in Widowland,
pretending you don't care any more, don't care
How many years now have I been praying for detours
around the Christmas Holidays that crucify,
underline the incompletion, deepen the loneliness?
Yes, I'm reading ads for Connections again,
Prestige Introductions   even although I know
they all have only five men and three hundred women
on their "active" lists, the men all losers,
and the women all desperate.

Back when my husband first died and the children
were all young, I used to get dressed up sometimes
to go to the A & P
  "Always wear your spurs in case
  you meet a horse"
I used to say to them, to explain my high heels
and eye-liner   and the children would all laugh;
Single parent standing in the generation gap
  that was when I still believed
I never gave up   dancing lessons, singles groups,
boring parties attended with one single hope
clubs joined   candidates supported   trips taken
married cowards screened out   home in tears

"What's wrong with me?
  There must be something wrong with me."
  My god! The Big Five O!

where are the match-makers amongst my friends
　　　　or even enemies?
past the promiscuous period
　　the alcoholic period
　　　　the last menstrual period
the psychiatrist period
　　(having insight into yourself only narrows the field further)
all the King's Weak Men arrive on my doorstep
following the scent of my strength growing stronger
I'm branded with "mother-surrogate"
　　　　they see it　　　　three miles off,
　　　　　　through cocktail party jungles
I mourn my waste　　　　already on deeper levels
armed on the invisible battlefield
　　　　I am turning to work
hope dies as more and more others
　　　　crowd into Widowland

often now I prison my hair in a bun
　　　　go numb to any body changes
even although I know I could still dance all night
if I do not now what day of the week it is
　　　　I bypass Saturday Night Outs

the children, watching, will never know
　　　　when the light in my eyes changed
in time even I will forget
　　when I took on the heaviness that cannot be shaken,
when reaching out
　　was finally put on ice,
the longings strangled, amputated
　　　　　　O Happy Happy New Year!
closet shame
　　　　unmateable

AT THE KINGSTON SHOPPING CENTRE

In the old dim stuffy
fast-food smelly shopping-centre,
spring stalemated,
I sat on a bench, waiting
for a friend
who was having her hair done

and listened in on the world
of school drop-outs,
bumming cigarettes,
sucking Pepsi;
of sad single mothers on welfare,
killing time;
of depressed and neutered old men,
retired to the benches,
and dying of it

three of them behind me,
one well-dressed,
in voices testosterone diminished
were arguing - as you would expect -
hockey

you know, the usual -
whether or not Wayne Gretsky
is the greatest,
whether or not Allan Eagleson
has lawyers smart enough
to get him off

suddenly they were approached
by someone familiar to them,
a deep voice greeting them,
"Joe, Phil, Ed,"
I turned sideways to look
and beheld a huge maple burl of a man,
seventies, maybe eighties,
leaning on a cane.

"Like to sit down, Jack?"
the well-dressed one said,
offering up his seat on the bench.

"No, thanks. I can still stand,"
Jack roared out
at the Grim Reaper
standing invisible
behind the bench

"Did you get into Rideaucrest, Jack?"

one of the others asked him,
giant gnarled working-man's hands,
turned a little purple,
old navy blue winter jacket
with hood, three sweaters
and a tie

"Well, hell! I don't know if I want
to get into Rideaucrest!
I don't want to give them
all my money
and I don't want to take orders.

I've taken orders all my life,
from my mother and father,
from my teachers at school,
from the army sergeants
in "The War to End All Wars,"
from my wife -
god rest her soul -
and I'll be goddamned
if at this stage of my life
I'm going somewhere where
it's all orders

get up at this time
eat at this time
poop at this time
bathe at this time
sleep at this time.

No thanks

I want to be free
to go out when I want to,
to have a beer when I want to,
see the Senators when I want to -
even if they haven't won a game
in two years -
Jesus! I've known steady losses
in my lifetime, too ---

He laughed and swung off
down the mall,
a huge maple burl of a man,
wading through the crowds

on his cane,
head and shoulders
above the mob of misguided "lookers,"
drifting like dried leaves
through the false-fronted emporium
of our times.

MOUTH-PAINTED, FOOT-PAINTED

Mouth-painted, foot-painted, they tumble
onto my desk and into my life annually,
disturbing reminders of Lady Luck's vagaries,
chain letters transmitted by a pernicious technology
from the Gethsemane of torn and mangled people.

I ask you, what have you or I ever done
with ourselves, perfectly whole and idiotically oblivious,
that compares with this projection of passion,
this unshakeable stipulation of will,
this resurrection of creative force
from the multi-fingered terrors of human beings
trampled, crumpled, disfigured, blinded,
legless, armless, yet with heightened humanity,
sharpened spirituality in their refusal
to submit, cower, lie down, quit and be carried?

Charles Ritchie, the famous Canadian diarist
once asked, "Why should only the famous
be remembered?"

And I say (with less authority, of course)
"Away with Abou Ben Adhem! Let Myron Anguses' name
lead all the rest!" His mouth-painted pain is pale,
stark, unpeopled. No one crosses on his country bridge,
snowed under on both sides of a grey river
where there is, as yet, no light
on his landscape, no bearable body image;
barren beauty is part of his lonely way back.

But January sunlight illuminates
the shadows that fill the farmyard
of T.C. Wells, where, whole again with a loved one,
proudly he rides forth
on some remembered prize-winning horseflesh,
the graveyard adjacent almost buried,
in the snows of a happy day when athletic limbs
and strength were taken for granted;
now the painter draws with his eyes,
not his hands.

Here are the twirling-in-ecstasy skaters
on Guilemette's pond, recalling lords of adolescence
before the drunk driver spewed young bodies
across the urban game of road hockey,
and stirred in young people the early wish to die.
We know who the skaters are, but who is the old man
walking down the road on two strong legs?

This Christmas Garland by an armless wonder named F. Bunn,
with a paint brush in his mouth,
ground down by his gritted teeth,
is greater in the eyes of God
than anything you or I have created,
ever will create, with all our limbs intact,
all our talents streaming forth and wasted,
all our potential unexplored, unused,
all our originality squandered.

These two rosy-cheeked and robust children,
ringing in the disabled Christmas of R. Christensen,
are they the son and daughter he can
no longer enfold within his missing arms,

and so he turns his grief to gladdening
your life, if only for a brief moment,
to showing the world how beautiful the children
he fathered in the days of his immortality?

Is not this Christmas card a statement
from a super being?

Some artist named A. Dale, double-jointed,
has foot-painted an ancestral horse and cutter
trotting through a white Christmas towards
the Christmas concert in the little church
nestled in the safety of his childhood's
carolling, and unaccompanied singing;
the road is winding, the snow drifts deep,
but the church glows with light
at the end of the tunnel.

Regressive, childlike, with muscular memory
L.J. Parker is Remembering the Farm
in wintertime when the roads were closed;
his purple mountains loom above red barns
and the farmhouse where we all began;
colour and archetypal form
are all he can deal with yet
in re-creation of his shattered world
discovery of his own unique source of will,
his imperfect beginning again, rebirth.

The soul of Toro Vatela blazes forth
from the manger in the humble stable
at Bethlehem where the newborn
dazzles the proud donkey,
glorifies the curious cattle,
astonishes the gentle lambs.

Tora Vatela mouth-paints the Nativity Scene
with new eyes, 20/20 vision born of tragedy;
he took a paint brush in his teeth one day,
intending to give to the four-limbed
proliferating chaos of our electrified world
his masterpiece of soothing peace and hope.

Seeing clear, not cybernetics, is everything.

The Winter Walk

Now snowy sleep the pyramidal pines, amidst the birch;
the wind, through rustling maples, stalks the road
whereon we walk although you lie, he who was uncontainable,
beside your ancestral Valley clan of Irish,
fastened down in marble-topped and regimented rows.

Always hopeful, the pileated woodpecker
makes his swooping loops, his shaggy forays,
in search of dead, not waiting, trees;
in secret woodland caves the sleeping bears
lie and hug together, cosy in their winter furs,
as I once curled with you, and would again.

Now lies my country road, snow-carved in Canada,
as all my life runs on in gratitude for you.

The elm survivors hold their icy fingertips
all Danae to the sky, waving diamond wands
over a frigid fairyland, coaxing sun
as your love breaks barriers, bends over me.

Now comes the virtuous vice of wintertime
as comes your life-in-death each day to me.

Oh, should I here rejoice that earth once shook
with your passage through seasons of committed passion?
Or should I grieve that all my love, empowered
by your love, cannot free you from this final frost,
yes, though I rain down my tears, smile upon you
as at our first meeting, implore you, reach out
to the resurrection of your arms outstretched--?

Now lies the first winter upon our love;
ice bridges the river of our separation,
snow entombs the lane of our laughing
all the way home; yet, as music exalts the soul,
so your love enfolds, succours, transforms,
exalts me and the remainder of my life,
fortifies me on this part of the journey,
the winter walk.

For I have loved and been loved, finally know now
how frail the snows, how ineffectual the ice.

POEMS FOR THE NEW TYRANNY

I ᴔ

Four Strong Winds   oh
and Lying in the Arms
of Mary   the songs
drop a plumb-line into a
Rubicon of universal

remorse   but oh
the new poems must look
into the fringed eye-

pit of passion   oh
they must   or Apple
will

(three oh's do now a poem
make   Canadian)

II ᴔ

Toothily, I had a tall tale
to reinforce the early back-
side of language

it was to be xeroxed
for the critics, a school
of Harvard-trained

fish
gasping for literary air

but before I got to   oh
the photo-copier

Chernobyl fall-out
(in An Early Morning Rain)
had blurred the copy

and posterity was

further impoverish-
ed

||| ↝

Before Yuppie Yoga   yes,
pre Gulf Oil's diversification into
                    Canadian porno magazines
the young computer programmer
suspected
                    in Ottawa
he had fallen in love with a Mi-
                    tel Marketer
verily, he serenaded her with computer
print-out sonnets
                              darker
than dark
          and laid
software gifts at her
shiny feet
          when she eloped
with a Gypsy Rover who rode
through Kanata one day when all
the power failed
                    in a Valley

storm

his back-up relief
was the clack
                and the click
the reassuring punctual soothing
flash
        the perfect
synchronization
                there,
havened in con-
        summate
                emptiness,
his palms sweated, his heart
stalled   mid-air   and he
experienced
        antiseptically
an unprecedented hard-
on

SUMMER RAIN AT HAMBLY LAKE

Turn off the Three Tenors!
let the rain make
its rarest of music
on my tin roof

The leaves outside
my screened porch
are like young birds
with their mouths open

The little house sits
on the uplands,
like a moist mushroom,
quietly breathing immobility,
with convoluted secrets
under its dome

I know this rain.
I know this rain so well.
It comes up from the lake,
across the old meadow
I guard and keep
for meadow's sake

After the long harsh
soul-destroying summer drought
the thrivers are those
who have deep roots,
drew water
from a hidden source

But some, alas,
will be late bloomers
with no time to seed
before the snows come

Sunny yesterday
when I looked up
from my work
there was a cerulean warbler
ablaze on the bladderwort

Last night
around my lake house
in the firefly fields
the wild white phlox
by moonlight
watched the falling stars

All day long
in my neighbour's fields
I could hear
the sheep feed,
quietly as stones

Now the rain
rains holiness
upon us,
unprayed for

If we all stood steady
in the rain like hemlock
or angelic birch
would we grow into harmony
with home, our earth?

Or, better still,
would we grow
until we died?

As the rain subsides
the robins remember
in their throats
they belong
to the thrush family

the fields grown old
in ancient grasses,
the meadow kept
for meadow's sake,
the tended gardens
round my little house,
all have never been
so beautiful, I think
except for that summer
a death ago
when you were here

LAST MISSION

What is left of him
is holding onto the wall
with the same hands
that dropped the bombs

There is no ounce of flesh left
to keep up the braces
on his Fighter Pilot
will to live,
(on the pants he dropped
so often in response
to the dirty Air Force ditty,
"Roll me over,
lay me down,
and do it again")

His face is shovelled out
but the eyes,
steady in second sight,
still snapping calculations,
retain the night vision
that flew sixty-three missions
over incarcerated Europe
in Wellingtons and Spitfires
to save democracy
for his country Canada

Sixty years of the rest of his life
he lived fuelled by ragings
that so few appreciated,
by anger so few remembered,
("Goddamnittohell
on one run
only twelve
of eighty-two
returned to base")

Now, brave airman,
going down into enemy-fired flames
(yet gentled by the prospect
of a final bonding
with the land he loved
and was prepared to die for).

Oh, ye of such diminished vision
and such shrivelled worlds,
get up from your push-button relaxers
and salute his final mission
as he crosses the Channel,
shot to ribbons,
out of gas,
singing homewards.
"Roll outthe barrel
and we'll have a barrel
of fun."

The Tigers of Sundarbans

On the Bay of Bengal,
along the coasts of India and Bangladesh,
live the tigers of Sundarbans;

related to the Royal Bengal Tigers,
the Sundarbans tigers do not obey
the same rule by which tigers elsewhere
govern their lives of stealth and duty;

anomalies, they eat people,
men who have gone into the jungle
to gather fuel,
travellers from one village
to another,
fishermen fishing in boats,
silently leaped upon
and devoured

Vidhaba Pallis, the tiger-widow villages
are filled with the family survivors
of men dispatched in tiger feasting

But do the people of the Sundarbans
set out to eradicate from the face of the earth
the singular man-eater?

Do the people of the Sundarbans
ride out in fanatic posses,
freighted with guns and ammunition,

loaded with tunnel vision,
infested with self-mutilating revenge,
to eradicate every beast in sight,
to destroy every magnificent animal
that kills for fun,
to unsettle the balance of their universe,
designated low-level, Third World
by the countries of the Great White hunters?

Not at all.
The man-eater is honoured
as the Forest Guardian

Far from the savage maws of great Western Cities
devouring their homeless lost children,
continents and epochs removed
from salivating slobbering Wal-Marts,
out of reach of the omnivorous jaws
of Western Technology,

the people of the Sundarbans in India
sanction their government's protection
of the man-eating tiger gliding through
his mangrove forest

with undamaged instincts,
not yet obliterated by Western Materialism,
with defining mysticism
they guard earth's delicate balance
for their children and their grandchildren

Tiger, tiger burning bright
in those enlightened forests
of the night.

SOME CONSOLATION

I hear you have had to fold up
your dream,
and put it in a trunk
like a wedding dress,
or old mining stock,
kept "just in case."

Word came over the treetops
from Toronto to Ottawa
to me here at the lake;
your news hollowed out
a place for itself
in my day

I have been away
working on a dream myself-
yes, another one!-
and weeds and wilderness
have taken over the gardens here.

So, at this delicate time
try to remember
carrots love tomatoes.

CONFESSION

And I have said to you I am always in reverence before your spirit;
I have spoken to you often about leaving your savage kingdom;
I have told you incestuous tribal tales you do not believe;
Yes, I have often cursed you for your Celtic incorrigibility.

I confess I have failed you, even betrayed you,
but who else in your life has cried in the night for you
and your broken dreams?
In strange and far-off places I have suddenly longed again
to have seen you as a young boy, as a young man;
Betimes, under the eaves in the rain-proof dark
after making love, or after you have been sick unto death,
I have kissed your holy hands and eyes
and promised you that we will meet hereafter.

Since our beginnings
I have always cared for your beginnings
and your endings.

Everyone knows
you are my blind spot,
and my second sight.

LOVE INTHE SILENT SONGLESS FIELDS

Love, in the silent songless fields of fall
I can hear the echoes of your voice
saying to me again, "We do not go
to hell by deed or choice
but by our stubborn repeated failure
to praise and rejoice."

I would like to go to a foreign country
to mourn in the coming night
our no longer standing together,
blended curves and height,
yet close enough to bare our fangs,
and turn, and fight.

I would like to go to a foreign country
put continents and seas between
the empty places at the foot
of the Mountains of Sheen
where you and I, winning and losing,
for so long loving have been.

The gate is closed on our laneway now,
our house will be locked and still,
the Lorrigidons will have taken over
the swamp at Holden's Hill;
Now I must pass through the songless fields
alone, and in the grace of our love, I will.

Notes to the Poems *For My Grandchildren*

1. Amy Lowell
2. Jung
3. Read
4. McLuhan
5. McLuhan
6. Jung
7. Finnigan
8. Peck
9. Einstein

ABOUT THE AUTHOR

Joan Finnigan has been at the forefront of literature in Canada since the 1960s. She was born and raised in Ottawa, and educated at Lisgar Collegiate, Carlton and Queen's universities; has been a teacher, and a reporter for the Ottawa Journal. During the sixties and seventies she did outstanding work for both CBC radio and the National Film Board, including her Genie-winning NFB screenplay, The Best Damn Fiddler from Calabogie to Kaladar. Her two most recent poetry collections, The Watershed Collection, 1998, and Wintering Over, 1992, were shortlisted for the Pat Lowther poetry Prize and the Trillium Award respectively

AGMV
MARQUIS
Québec, Canada
1998